Big Tree
little

Story by Sylvia
Pictures by Suzanna Ros

LION PUBLISHING

'We learned a new song in school today,' said Daren to his Mum as he ate his tea. 'One about God making the sky and the trees. But it's not really true, is it,' he said, 'that bit about God making the trees?'

He looked down, out of the window, to the windswept courtyard far below, then beyond the flats to the park.

'When did he make that tree—that big one in the middle of the park?' he asked.

'That old oak tree?' said Mum. I should think he's been slowly making that tree for about two hundred years. Oak trees are slow growers.'

'Two hundred years!' exclaimed Daren. 'That's older than you and Dad, isn't it?' he said.

'Just a bit,' said Mum.

'But how did God start making the tree?' asked Daren. 'Did people just wake up one day, and there it was?'

'You go and find me your anorak, and I'll show you how God started to make that oak tree,' said Mum.

'My anorak?' said Daren.

'Yes,' said Mum.

Looking puzzled, Daren hunted for his anorak.

'Now turn out the pockets, and show me what you've got,' said Mum.

'Two marbles, a dirty hanky, a bus ticket, a bit of chewed gum and an acorn,' said Daren.

'Ah! It's the acorn I want,' said Mum. 'I saw you pick it up the other day in the park. Now that's what God starts with when he begins to make an oak tree.'

Daren looked at the dull brown acorn in surprise.

'An oak tree starts with an acorn?' he said. 'How?'

'We can watch and find out — but God works very slowly sometimes, so you will have to be patient.' Mum went to the cupboard and hunted for a while. 'Here, this will do,' she said.

It was a small bottle. 'Fill it with water, please, Daren.'

When Daren had filled it with water, Mum put the acorn in at the top of the bottle. The tip of the acorn was just touching the water.

'Now put it on the window-sill, and we'll look at it every day and see what happens,' she said.

That night, when Dad came home from work, Daren told him about the acorn.

'We're going to watch God make an oak tree,' Daren said.

'You'll be an old man before it's finished,' Dad laughed. But when he said prayers with Daren that night he said, 'Please God, help Daren's acorn grow into a big oak tree.'

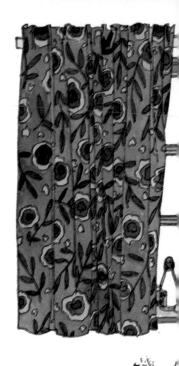

Next morning,
Daren jumped out of
bed and ran to the
window-sill.
    'Nothing's happened, Mum!'
he called out.

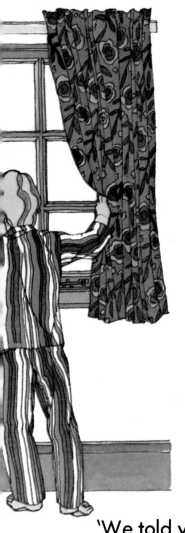

'God hasn't made an oak tree like you said he would.'
     'We told you you would have to be patient,' Dad called back.

Every day Daren looked at the acorn. At last one morning he called out excitedly.

'Hey! Mum! Look, it's begun to grow!' From the bottom of the acorn, a small shoot had sprouted.

'That is the first root growing,' said Mum. 'It is very strong. You see — it will fill the bottle before long.'

Every day the root had grown a little longer. It had to curl round to fit in the bottle. But no leaves grew at the top and no branch showed there.

'That takes longer to come,' said Dad. 'But if you lift the acorn gently from the bottle, you will see that something is happening.'

Daren lifted up the acorn. He was careful not to break the curly root. The brown skin was cracking off the acorn. Under the skin, the acorn was turning from cream to bright scarlet. It was also beginning to split at the bottom, and a tiny new shoot was showing.

'That is the stem coming,' said Mum. 'one day it will be a thick tree trunk.'

Several weeks later, the tiny shoot had grown upwards into a thin stem, as tall as Daren's hand. At the top were two bronze-coloured leaves.

'Now you can begin to see it looking really like an oak tree,' said Mum.

Daren looked across to the great oak in the park. Could his little tree really grow as big as that?

'What shall we do with our tree now?' he said. 'The root has filled the bottle and needs more room. Soon it will be so tall, it will topple over.'

'Why not ask your friend Carly if we can plant it in her garden? She doesn't live in a flat like us.'

Carly was very excited at the idea of planting an oak tree in her garden. Her Mum said it had better go in the corner, where the dog wouldn't dig it up.

'It's very tiny,' said Carly. 'Is it really an oak tree?'

'Yes,' said Daren. 'God's going to take hundreds of years to make it grow into a really big one.'

'When it's bigger we can climb in it and build a tree house,' said Carly.

'Cor! Yes!' said Daren.

Carly's Mum and Daren's Mum smiled at each other.